Santa Muerte Devotion 101

Answers and Explanations

for Curious Readers and New Devotees

By: Arnold Bustillo

SantaMuerteMagick.com

Table of Contents

Introduction

The Santa Muerte, as she is known today, is a relatively new phenomenon. Despite the fact that the number of her devotees continues to grow, there remains to be much confusion over how to practically approach Santa Muerte. As someone who owns a website dedicated to the practice of Santa Muerte magick (www.SantaMuerteMagick.com), I get emails all the time from people asking me whether or not the urban legends they've heard are true. Many of the emails I get come from people who seem genuinely scared about approaching the Santa Muerte, and some who want to know whether or not they will be doomed to some terrible fate after asking the Santa Muerte for help. Personally, I think the Santa Muerte is the kindest, most loving energy you could ever approach.

I first met the Santa Muerte in Tijuana, Mexico, where I lived for many years, between 2016 and 2022. My mother had retired to the border city, and after visiting the city for myself, I decided to stay (I was a bit of a nomad at the time). It was during the first couple of days of my arrival in Tijuana that I noticed all the depictions of what I mistakenly believed to be the Grim Reaper. I asked my mother about the depictions, and she proceeded to explain to me that the statues and altars of the cloaked skeleton were not the Grim Reaper, but the Santa Muerte, or Saint Death, a Mexican folk saint with the power to destroy whatever stands in the way of what you want.

I was immediately fascinated. I devoured any information I could find on the saint. I purchased Spanish language booklets sold in the local *botanicas* (spiritual supply shops), and visited her public altars to watch how the locals interacted with the Skeleton Saint, as she is sometimes called. I read any book and watched any video that I could find about her. The more I learned, the more I came to love and understand the Santa Muerte. Eventually I found myself joining the locals by making offerings at the public altars, and even constructing a personal altar of my own in the Tijuana apartment where I lived.

During the time that I was living in Tijuana, I worked primarily as a freelance writer for American businesses in need of marketing and blog content. When I would make offerings to the Santa Muerte, I would ask that she smile upon my efforts in business and that she would send me clients who would buy my work. Today, most of what I write is dedicated to spreading knowledge about the Santa Muerte, and helping people understand her as much as possible. I like to think that the Santa Muerte saw promise in my abilities as a writer and decided to put me to work as a writer for her growing community of devotees.

Which brings me to this book that you're reading right now. This book was inspired by all the questions I've received through my website. Hopefully it does a good job of answering some of the questions you might have, and gives you a foundation from which you can start on your own path of Santa Muerte devotion.

What Is the Santa Muerte?

The Santa Muerte is death.

She is not a spirit or deity with dominion over death, but the personification of death itself. This distinction is important because spirits and deities are themselves subject to the power of death. When all the believers of a god disappear, so too does that god die. The Santa Muerte, on the other hand, is a constant force that exists whether or not you believe in her. She is a fact of life that does not require belief in order to be made real. If all the devotees of Santa Muerte were to suddenly disappear, she would not lose any of her power, because human beings are not the only things alive in the universe. In fact, the very universe we call home is itself alive, which means that it will one day succumb to Santa Muerte as well, at which point a new beginning will be born. Since every death gives way to a new beginning, and since every new beginning must one day die, then it becomes clear that the power of Santa Muerte is perpetual and never-ending.

The idea of Santa Muerte as we know her today, comes from Mexico. Obviously, death does not just exist in Mexico, but we do have the Mexicans to thank for helping to thrust Santa Muerte onto the world stage and teaching the rest of the world how to spiritually approach the Skeleton Saint. If the continent we call Afirca is the cradle of humankind as we know it today, then the area we call Mexico is the cradle of Santa Muerte as we know her today.

In seeking to understand what is the Santa Muerte, it's also important to understand a bit about the Spanish language. The language itself is gendered, so words are either masculine or feminine. "Santa" is the feminine form of the word "Saint", so it's fair to say that, in Mexico, death is a woman. Many words in Spanish, like other languages, can carry more than one meaning. While "Santa" is the feminine form of the word "Saint", it can also be translated to mean "Holy", which reflects and embodies the spiritual, and even magickal, aspects of death. If death was simply the end of physical life, then there would be nothing to pray to. The holiness of death is what allows us to pray to Santa Muerte for miracles and to seek her magickal blessings.

Finally, "Santa", as a derivative of "Holy," can also be translated to mean "Good". When we devote ourselves to Santa Muerte, we are therefore devoting ourselves to a "Good Death". There are many ways to die, and many ideas of what constitutes a good death. For some, a good death is a quick death, experienced as painlessly as possible. For others, a good death is a comfortable death in a familiar place and surrounded by loved ones. What does a good death mean to you? When we devote ourselves to Santa Muerte, we are ultimately asking for the best death possible - whatever that may be to us.

Who May Be a Devotee of Santa Muerte?

We are all welcome to be devotees of Santa Muerte.

If you are alive, then you will one day die, and it is this fact which connects every human being on the planet to the Santa Muerte. While you may not consider yourself a devotee as of yet, and while there are even people who actively avoid acknowledging the power of Santa Muerte, the fact is that she is coming for us all, and each day that we live to see, each breath that we live to breathe, is one small step that takes us ever closer to her impending embrace.

One reason why the community of Santa Muerte devotees continues to grow is precisely because of how accepting the Santa Muerte is. She is a force accessible and approachable by all of us. Often depicted with the scales of justice, the Santa Muerte is frequently described as The Great Equalizer, because nobody gets special treatment. No matter how good you are, no matter how many mistakes you make, the Santa Muerte will come for you, too. Where some gods might reject you for who you love, or for where you come from, the Santa Muerte is completely indifferent.

Mexico might be the cradle of Santa Muerte, but you don't have to be Mexican to know death. Death exists in all cultures and all religions, so you can be from any culture and of any religion (or no religion at all), and the Santa Muerte will accept you.

If you have ever been made to feel as if a certain spiritual path was out of your reach because you didn't have the right skin color, the right lineage, or the right initiatory degrees, then rest easy knowing there's a place for you as a devotee of Holy Death. Santa Muerte has no skin, so race is of no importance to her. Santa Muerte has accepted all of our dead ancestors, so a lineage is already shared. Santa Muerte has been moving towards each of us since we were born, so it was our birth that initiated us into her community.

Are Santa Muerte Devotees Obsessed with Death?

To the inexperienced outsider, it may appear as if Santa Muerte devotees have an unnatural obsession with death. This could not be farther from the truth. Many of us may love the Halloween season above all others, and some of us might have an affinity for dark and quiet places, but the fact is that devotion to Santa Muerte is just as much about life as it is about death.

When we acknowledge death, dress it up in cloaks of different colors and adorn its altar with fruits and flowers and booze, we acknowledge the finite nature of life, which in turn reminds us to cherish whatever life we have remaining. When we are able to come to terms with the fact that everything we love about this Earth will one day come to an end, it puts us on notice that we must live life on our terms, right here and right now. We must spend as much time as we can with the people that we love, and we must spend as much time as we can indulging in life's physical pleasures.

Devotion to Santa Muerte is about the acknowledgement of death, the facing of death head on, rather than the avoidance of it. Death is not something that can be avoided, and facing it head on can be amazingly liberating. Make no mistake, death is coming for you. Every breath you take only brings you closer to death's final embrace. You can try to ignore this fact and pretend that you will have forever to get around to the things that make you happy, but you will only be disappointed in the end. From this point of view, it would be fair to characterize Santa Muerte devotees not as obsessed with death, but as obsessed with life.

Is Santa Muerte
a Saint of Criminals?

Yes.

But she's also a saint of homemakers and a saint of breadwinners. She's a saint of children and a saint of parents. She's a saint of artists and a saint of soldiers.

Remember that Santa Muerte accepts us all - and since there are criminals among us, then Santa Muerte would, by default, also be a criminal's saint. One reason why some criminals pray to Santa Muerte is precisely because she does not judge them. She does not hold their bad choices against them and promises to always accept them.

We are not puppets of the Santa Muerte, and we each exist with independent agency and free will. For the most part, it would seem like the Santa Muerte allows us to go about our business here on Earth, and only interferes when (1) she wants to usher us into the afterlife, (2) when she feels like granting a petition, or (3) when she feels like sharing blessings with her devotees. For the rest of us who must share this world with criminals, note that this chapter does not seek to excuse the criminal behavior of devotees. Just as we each have the choice to obey the law or ignore it, we as a society also have the choice to implement and enforce consequences for those who choose to ignore our laws.

Will the Santa Muerte hear the petitions of professional criminals? Yes, because she hears all petitions. Will the Santa Muerte grant protection and success to criminals? Maybe, but death is a force that cannot be commanded, and the buck stops with Santa Muerte - only she will decide what petitions are granted, and for how long someone can get away with living a criminal life. I like to think of Santa Muerte as a loving mother or grandmother. Just as our mothers and grandmothers will always love us, no matter how much we screw up, even those that love us can get tired of bailing us out and decide to let us learn our lessons the hard way. Considering the relatively short lifespan of career criminals, it would appear that even Santa Muerte eventually gets tired of criminal antics.

Perhaps the biggest mistake anyone can make is to judge an entire community on the actions of those on the criminal fringes. There are members of the Italian and Irish mafias who wear crosses and identify as Catholic. There are members of the Japanese yakuza who pray to ancestors and nature spirits and identify as followers of Shinto. Is Jesus the reason why Italian and Irish mobsters kill people? Are the ancestors and nature spirits the reasons why the yakuza kill people? Of course not. These are criminal organizations made up of people from specific regions. It is the people in these organizations that bring their spiritual beliefs into their criminal behavior, it is not the spiritual beliefs that spawn the criminal behavior. Mexican criminal organizations consist of Mexicans - Santa Muerte as we know her today was born from Mexico. A group of Mexicans praying to a Mexican folk saint is not a sign of inherent criminality - it's basic sociology.

Can Atheists be Devotees of Santa Muerte?

Yes.

An atheist is often defined as one who does not believe in the existence of any gods. It is more accurate to say, however, that an atheist is one who is unconvinced by the assertions made by theists in regard to whether or not god(s) exist(s). No matter how you choose to define atheism, there is no argument against an atheist becoming a devotee of Santa Muerte.

Remember that Santa Muerte is death itself - I don't think there is any atheist among us who could refute the existence of death. Where gods die when there is nobody left to believe in them, death thrives even in the absence of belief.

Readers who have followed my work may be surprised to learn that I myself came to Santa Muerte devotion from a position of atheism. In fact, I still consider myself an atheist - that is one who is unconvinced by the god claims made by theists. When I served as a Humvee driver during combat operations in Baghdad, I saw absolutely no evidence for the existence of any god, but was inundated with proof for the existence of death. It was not until I met Santa Muerte in Tijuana, Mexico that I realized even without a god to call my own, I could still explore spirituality and find spiritual fulfillment in the arms of Holy Death.

Is there a god? I don't know, and neither does anybody else.

Is there death? Yes, absolutely. She does not need your belief in order to be made real and every intellectually honest adult on Earth, spiritual or not, would agree wholeheartedly that each and every one of us will one day experience death.

Benefits of
Santa Muerte Devotion

Devoting yourself to any spiritual path just because of what you stand to gain by following that path is a recipe for disaster, because as soon as the spiritual path fails to deliver what you want, you're all the more likely to walk away from the path in frustration. Rather than devoting yourself to a spiritual path for what it can do for you, it is better to devote yourself to one that not only serves you, but the people around you, as well as the path itself.

In my experience, the Santa Muerte seems to smile on devotees who spread their blessings around, rather than hoarding them. For example, when I was living in Tijuana asking Santa Muerte for clients who would buy my work, I usually spent the money I earned by supporting my mother, who needed my help at the time. Even now that I write books and blog posts about the Santa Muerte, I write them not only so they may provide income that keeps me alive and comfortable, but also so that I may help to bring more people into this growing community of Santa Muerte devotees.

This being said, devotees who approach Santa Muerte with a kind and unselfish heart do appear to experience a variety of benefits. One of the major benefits of Santa Muerte devotion is spiritual fulfillment. To be spiritually fulfilled is to feel comfortable on your spiritual path. The problem with many modern religions is the amount of shame and condemnation which is built into those spiritual systems. How can people feel fulfilled when they are taught that they must subjugate themselves, be ashamed of themselves, and hide themselves from the world? As devotees of Santa Muerte, we are all seen as equals, we are allowed to experience the world, and we are not made to be ashamed of who we are. Even before we give ourselves to Santa Muerte devotion, we are accepted by Santa Muerte, which means we can be free to explore our individual spiritual paths, and the world around us, without constantly worrying that we will somehow sin against or anger the Santa Muerte.

Another benefit which can be gained through devotion to Santa Muerte is the ability to accept your own mortality. Once you face your mortality and come to terms with the fact that your life will one day end, and there is nothing you can do about it, then all that is sweet in the world is made more sweet, and all that is bitter in the world is made less bitter. When you accept that your life will one day end, you will appreciate and savor things like good food, good sex, and sunny days. Likewise, when you accept that your life will one day end, you will feel less depressed about pain and suffering.

Santa Muerte devotion also allows you to enter into a community of fellow devotees. Devotees of death exist all over the world and come from all walks of life. While you may not always like how another has chosen to live life, the fact that we are all equal under Santa Muerte means you should at least respect all others and come to the aid of other devotees whenever possible.

What Problems Does Santa Muerte Help With?

Any problems you can think of.

Part of the reason why the following of Santa Muerte is growing so much is because she will hear all petitions without judgment against those who make the petitions. From the restoration of health to a sexual fling with a married man, there is nothing that we can't ask the Santa Muerte to deliver. The Santa Muerte may be asked to deliver a blessing just as easily as she can be asked to deliver a curse against an enemy. Where major religions see the world in black and white and may hold it against the person asking for something like a curse to an enemy, or for protection in a criminal enterprise, the Santa Muerte understands that the world is full of shades of gray, and therefore considers each petition on its own merits.

If a devotee has a strong relationship with Santa Muerte, it is very possible that Santa Muerte would grant a petition considered taboo by society. To the Santa Muerte, the matters of human beings are the matters of human beings. She is known to grant petitions, but she does not seem to concern herself with what is right and what is wrong by the standards of our human society - that's what human constructs are for, like the criminal justice system.

For example, a criminal may ask Santa Muerte to protect a shipment of illegal goods, and the Santa Muerte may decide to grant the petition, but it is not a guarantee that the police will not eventually catch up with the criminal on another day. Likewise, a person may ask Santa Muerte to deliver a sexual fling with a married man, but it's not a guarantee that the jilted spouse won't find out and want to seek revenge of her own. In other words - be careful what you ask for, because you just might get it.

The Afterlife
for Santa Muerte Devotees

It's only natural for human beings to wonder what will happen to us when we die. Unfortunately, the only people who can tell us what the afterlife is like are all dead.

For devotees of Santa Muerte, there is no afterlife myth, and many of us do not concern ourselves with what we cannot possibly know. Most religions seek to explain the unexplainable for no other reason than it makes people feel good, but making up a story when there is a hole in the facts doesn't change the facts - the facts are as they are - the story just becomes little more than a drug that helps people sleep at night. As devotees of Santa Muerte who choose to be honest with ourselves by acknowledging death, we must also be honest with ourselves and acknowledge that we do not know what we do not know. The truth will be revealed to us in good time, and there is nothing wrong with admitting our present ignorance.

Death is never an end, but a new beginning that we will all get to experience. New beginnings can be scary - this is the nature of the unknown. Rather than focusing on what you cannot know, on an idea of an afterlife that may or may not be correct, I would encourage you to instead focus on what you do know, like what you know about being a good person on this Earth, in the here and now.

How to Become a Santa Muerte Devotee

The secret to becoming a Santa Muerte devotee is that there is no secret. As already stated, the Santa Muerte accepts us all. If you are alive, then you will one day die, which means you are already growing closer to the Santa Muerte every day. The difference between a devotee of Santa Muerte and the rest of the world is only that the devotee acknowledges Santa Muerte, rather than trying to ignore her.

There are several ways to acknowledge Santa Muerte. Perhaps the easiest and most basic method is by praying to her, which only requires an open heart. There are many ways to pray, and there is no right or wrong way to do it. The prayers you choose to recite may be poetic and rhyming, or completely conversational. They may be written in advance by other devotees or improvised in the moment. Prayers may be recited to make a request of Santa Muerte, to give thanks to her, or simply to say hello.

Another way to acknowledge Santa Muerte is to build an altar to her. There will be more discussed on the topic of altars later, but the basic rule is that an altar should contain a depiction of Santa Muerte; which can either be a literal depiction, like a statue or a painting of Santa Muerte herself, or a symbolic depiction of death, like a plaster skull or an image of a skull and crossbones. The altar may be a permanent altar in your home, or a temporary altar that is disassembled and put away when not in use. When circumstances prevent a devotee from keeping a physical Santa Muerte altar, an altar may also be conjured within the mind's eye - a sort of astral altar, as I call it, which I have also referred to as "the altar in one's heart".

Santa Muerte may also be acknowledged through the making of offerings. Again, there is no doctrine as to what constitutes a good offering, but I tend to advise devotees that the offering should be something which you yourself would like to receive as a gift. At the heart of a good offering is sacrifice - we shouldn't give the Santa Muerte something just because we have nothing else to do with the item, there should be true thought behind the offering because, as with every gift you will give or receive, it truly is the thought that counts. More will be shared on the topic of offerings later; for now, I only want to introduce the idea as a way of acknowledging Saint Death.

When we acknowledge the Santa Muerte, either through prayers, constructing an altar, or making offerings, we show Santa Muerte that we are no longer ignoring her, and that we wish to form a relationship with her. The more we acknowledge Santa Muerte, the stronger that relationship will become. This is important, especially for those who wish to petition the Santa Muerte for magickal favors, because it is the relationship with Santa Muerte which is the foundation for magickal success.

Remember that Santa Muerte has already decided that we are all worthy of her embrace, evidenced by the fact that we are all alive and therefore getting closer to death every day. Because of this, there is no switch that needs to be flipped in order to become a devotee - no test or initiation that needs to be completed. While it is true that you may perform a ritual to mark the beginning of your devotion to Santa Muerte, it would be a ritual performed voluntarily, rather than to satisfy some requirement of Santa Muerte.

Your devotion to Santa Muerte begins the first day you say a prayer to her, build an altar to her, or make an offering to her. Every prayer, altar, or offering that comes to follow is a reinforcement of your devotion, in order to strengthen your relationship with her.

How to Pray to Santa Muerte

Prayer is one of the ways that we acknowledge Santa Muerte to show that we are devoted to her and wish to build a relationship with her. Prayer, however, is a deeply personal process, and there is no right or wrong way to do it. Most religions have some physical method of prayer, like the Christians who clasp their hands and lower their heads, or the Muslims who kneel and bow, but there is no doctrine for Santa Muerte devotees which dictates how devotees must pray to her.

Remember that Santa Muerte accepts us all, and this includes those of us who follow one religion or another. Because of this, devotees of Santa Muerte who are also followers of a particular religion may pray to Santa Muerte using the rules of prayer dictated by their own religion. This is why it is common to see

Santa Muerte devotees in Mexico, which is a Catholic majority country, praying to Santa Muerte in much the way that Catholics pray to Jesus and the Virgin Mary.

For those devotees who are not members of organized religions, or those who wish to leave their old religions behind, prayer to Santa Muerte is not something you should overthink. A simple way to pray to Santa Muerte is to close the eyes and speak the words which you want Santa Muerte to hear - the words may be spoken aloud, as whispers, or in your own head the way you might talk to yourself.

Prayer is a good way to ask the Santa Muerte for favors, and many Santa Muerte petition rituals will often involve some element of prayer, but getting something should not be the only reason why you pray. It is also possible to pray to Santa Muerte without asking for anything at all in return. For example, you could offer prayers of thanks for the blessings which Santa Muerte bestows on you, like the blessing of each day you are allowed to live, or prayers of invitation, like inviting Santa Muerte to be next to you on your morning walk.

What you decide to pray to Santa Muerte is also up to you. Some devotees make a plan for what they want to pray about, and others simply improvise as they go along. The prayers you recite may be poetic or conversational, they may be your own original words or words written by another person, like the prayers I share on my own website, SantaMuerteMagick.com. A prayer may be a single sentence, like, "I love you, Santa Muerte," or an entire collection of prayers, like the Santa Muerte Rosary, which is shared in the next chapter, and which can take up to a half hour to recite from beginning to end.

When you pray to Santa Muerte, the last piece of advice I have is to acknowledge the Santa Muerte in your prayer, so your intention of communicating with Santa Muerte is made clear. This can be accomplished the same way you might begin a letter to a friend, by acknowledging the friend by name at the top of the letter. In other words, you can start your prayer to Santa Muerte by simply saying, "Santa Muerte," and then continuing with whatever you want to say. You may also put your acknowledgement of Santa Muerte at the end of the prayer, by reciting something like "Thank you Santa Muerte," or even, "In your name, Santa Muerte, amen."

The Santa Muerte Rosary

The Santa Muerte Rosary is a collection of prayers recited by devotees for different reasons. You may recite the rosary as a form of meditation to clear the head and lift the spirits, or as an act of devotion, to acknowledge the Santa Muerte and show her that you are thinking of her. If you make a contract with Santa Muerte, which is explained later in the chapter "How to Make a Contract with Santa Muerte", you may also offer to recite the rosary in exchange for a miracle granted.

The term "rosary" refers not just to the prayers recited, but also to the physical collection of beads which may be held in the hands as you pray. A rosary typically includes 59 beads, a medallion of the Santa Muerte, and a three way connector which brings all the ends of the rosary together to form a necklace. You do not technically need a physical rosary in order to recite the rosary prayers, but the beads are quite helpful for keeping track of your place as you move through the recitation.

What follows is a complete Santa Muerte rosary prayer as it would be recited from beginning to end. You are free to recite only parts of the rosary, for example to adapt your favorite lines into morning or evening prayers, but the entire rosary is shared here so you may decide how best to incorporate the prayers into your Santa Muerte devotion. All of the prayers presented here are my own original creation, but you should feel free to adapt any of the lines of the prayers, or the order and frequency of the prayers in the rosary, for your own personal use.

If using a physical rosary necklace, simply start at the medallion and move up the necklace one bead at a time, reciting the appropriate prayer or set of prayers that correspond to each point on the rosary. Go up one side of the necklace and down the other until all beads have been covered by the appropriate prayer or set of prayers. The last point on the rosary necklace, the place that marks the recitation of the "Closing Prayer" in the rosary, is the three way connector - the point on the rosary where the three ends of the rosary connect. The three way connector may or may not be marked by a bead, but if it is, then it is skipped at the beginning of the rosary and only counted at the very end of the rosary. See diagram that follows:

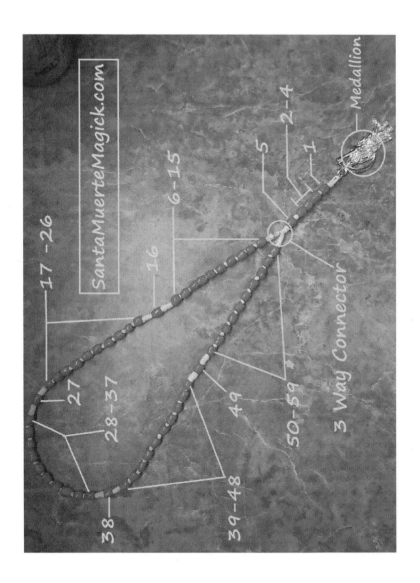

SantaMuerteMagick.com

17 -26
6-15
2-4
Medallion
5
1
16
27
28-37
38
39-48
49
50-59
3 Way Connector

To begin, hold the medallion or amulet depicting the image of the Santa Muerte in your hands and pray the following Santa Muerte Rosary "Opening Prayer":

"Santa Muerte, Holy Death,
I offer these prayers for you.
From the altar in my heart, to your ears,
may you find the words sweet, and their meanings true.
Santa Muerte, Holy Death,
I offer these prayers for you."

On bead 1, pray one "Our Santa Muerte":

"Our Santa Muerte who will come for us all,
kind and gentle be your kiss.
When you come to end my life,
may I be free of any regrets.
Thank you for this day, one more beautiful day,
so I may have it to live, love, and laugh my own way,
amen."

On beads 2-4, pray one "Glory Be Holy Death" each:
"Glory be Holy Death, blessed death, peaceful death.

47

As you have been with me from the beginning,

so are you with me now,

and so will you be with me always, amen."

On bead 5, pray the First Mystery of Santa Muerte:

"The Santa Muerte holds in her hand

a magick scythe she commands.

When at us her scythe does swing,

swift to us, our death she brings.

Our Santa Muerte who will come for us all,

kind and gentle be your kiss.

When you come to end my life,

may I be free of any regrets.

Thank you for this day, one more beautiful day,

so I may have it to live, love, and laugh my own way,

amen.

Hail the Santisima, full of love and grace.

Blessed by you are the forsaken and forgotten.

Blessed by you are the abused and downtrodden.

Hail the Santisima, who holds power over all,

bless us with your love

now and at the moment of our deaths, amen.

Glory be Holy Death, blessed death, peaceful death.
As you have been with me from the beginning,
so are you with me now,
and so will you be with me always, amen."

On bead 6 - 15, pray one "Hail the Santisima" each:

"Hail the Santisima, full of love and grace.
Blessed by you are the forsaken and forgotten.
Blessed by you are the abused and downtrodden.
Hail the Santisima, who holds power over all,
bless us with your love
now and at the moment of our deaths, amen."

On bead 16, pray the Second Mystery:

"On the back of Death is placed,
hooded cloak of magick great.
With this power Death protects,
each of us from birth to death.

Our Santa Muerte who will come for us all,

kind and gentle be your kiss.

When you come to end my life,

may I be free of any regrets.

Thank you for this day, one more beautiful day,

so I may have it to live, love, and laugh my own way,

amen.

Hail the Santisima, full of love and grace.

Blessed by you are the forsaken and forgotten.

Blessed by you are the abused and downtrodden.

Hail the Santisima, who holds power over all,

bless us with your love

now and at the moment of our deaths, amen.

Glory be Holy Death, blessed death, peaceful death.

As you have been with me from the beginning,

so are you with me now,

and so will you be with me always, amen."

On bead 17 - 26, pray one "Hail the Santisima" each:

"Hail the Santisima, full of love and grace.

Blessed by you are the forsaken and forgotten.

Blessed by you are the abused and downtrodden.

Hail the Santisima, who holds power over all,

bless us with your love

now and at the moment of our deaths, amen."

On bead 27, pray the Third Mystery:

"Balanced in Death's hand of bone,

scales of justice, to all shown.

Special treatment, none receive,

from this Earth, we all must leave.

Our Santa Muerte who will come for us all,

kind and gentle be your kiss.

When you come to end my life,

may I be free of any regrets.

Thank you for this day, one more beautiful day,

so I may have it to live, love, and laugh my own way,

amen.

Hail the Santisima, full of love and grace.

Blessed by you are the forsaken and forgotten.

Blessed by you are the abused and downtrodden.

Hail the Santisima, who holds power over all,

bless us with your love

now and at the moment of our deaths, amen.

Glory be Holy Death, blessed death, peaceful death.

As you have been with me from the beginning,

so are you with me now,

and so will you be with me always, amen."

On bead 28 - 37, pray one "Hail the Santisima" each:

"Hail the Santisima, full of love and grace.

Blessed by you are the forsaken and forgotten.

Blessed by you are the abused and downtrodden.

Hail the Santisima, who holds power over all,

bless us with your love

now and at the moment of our deaths, amen."

On bead 38, pray the Fourth Mystery:

"Santa Muerte walks the Earth,

those who love her, she will serve.

Fear not Death, be unafraid,

Death is with us, everyday.

Our Santa Muerte who will come for us all,

kind and gentle be your kiss.

When you come to end my life,

may I be free of any regrets.

Thank you for this day, one more beautiful day,

so I may have it to live, love, and laugh my own way,

amen.

Hail the Santisima, full of love and grace.

Blessed by you are the forsaken and forgotten.

Blessed by you are the abused and downtrodden.

Hail the Santisima, who holds power over all,

bless us with your love

now and at the moment of our deaths, amen.

Glory be Holy Death, blessed death, peaceful death.

As you have been with me from the beginning,

so are you with me now,

and so will you be with me always, amen."

On bead 39 - 48, pray one "Hail the Santisima" each:

"Hail the Santisima, full of love and grace.

Blessed by you are the forsaken and forgotten.

Blessed by you are the abused and downtrodden.

Hail the Santisima, who holds power over all,

bless us with your love

now and at the moment of our deaths, amen."

On bead 49, pray the Fifth Mystery:

"Land of living, land of dead,

at the bridge between stands Death.

When the flame of life is lost,

Santa Muerte helps us cross.

Our Santa Muerte who will come for us all,

kind and gentle be your kiss.

When you come to end my life,

may I be free of any regrets.

Thank you for this day, one more beautiful day,

so I may have it to live, love, and laugh my own way,

amen.

Hail the Santisima, full of love and grace.

Blessed by you are the forsaken and forgotten.

Blessed by you are the abused and downtrodden.

Hail the Santisima, who holds power over all,

bless us with your love

now and at the moment of our deaths, amen.

Glory be Holy Death, blessed death, peaceful death.

As you have been with me from the beginning,

so are you with me now,

and so will you be with me always, amen."

On bead 50 - 59, pray one "Hail the Santisima" each:

"Hail the Santisima, full of love and grace.

Blessed by you are the forsaken and forgotten.

Blessed by you are the abused and downtrodden.

Hail the Santisima, who holds power over all,

bless us with your love

now and at the moment of our deaths, amen."

Hold the three way connector in your hands and pray the following Santa Muerte Rosary "Closing Prayer":

"Hail to you Santa Muerte,

when to you I turn in desperation,

may you shine mercy upon me.

Hail to you Santa Muerte,

when to you I bring petition,

may you shine favor upon me.

Use your powers on my behalf,

and never forsake me,

Santisima Muerte, amen."

- The End

How to Build a Physical Santa Muerte Altar

For Santa Muerte devotees, an altar is a representation of our relationship with Holy Death. As stated earlier, a devotee is one who acknowledges Santa Muerte, and building an altar to Saint Death is one way that she can be acknowledged. One type of altar that you can build to Santa Muerte is a physical altar.

The only thing you need to make an altar to Santa Muerte is a depiction or representation of death. This can be a literal representation, such as a statue or painting of Santa Muerte, or a symbolic representation, such as a plaster skull or a sketch of a skull and crossbones. An altar to Santa Muerte can also be constructed covertly, or hidden in plain sight. Remember that Santa Muerte is death itself, so any representation of death can serve as the foundation for an altar to Santa Muerte. For example, a vase of dead flowers or a bowl of dead leaves can serve as the required representation of death, as could a trophy animal skull, the kind that would be mounted on a wall.

Other representations of death that can be used for a covert altar are representations of items associated with Santa Muerte, like the scythe or sickle (which represents Santa Muerte's power to cut the thread of life), the globe (which represents Santa Muerte's dominion over every living thing on Earth), the owl (which represents the wisdom of Santa Muerte and her knowledge of magick), the hourglass (which represents the finite nature of life), or the scales of justice (which represent the fact that we are all equal in the eyes of Santa Muerte).

If you were in a pinch, you could even draw a basic skull on a piece of paper and use that as the foundation for an altar. All that matters is that death is represented on your altar - how you choose to represent her is up to you.

When you have your depiction or representation of death, you can place it on whatever surface you have available. It doesn't matter where or how high you put your Santa Muerte altar, but you should place it with respect. This means the area should be clean and safe from random disturbances. You could place your altar up on a bookshelf or mantle, or directly on the floor in the corner of a room. My own altar, as I type these words, is on a section of kitchen counter, overlooking me as I work. Placing your depiction of death on some kind of altar cloth is also recommended, in order to distinguish where the altar begins and where it ends.

There are no size requirements when it comes to building a physical Santa Muerte altar. My very first Santa Muerte altar was anchored by a one inch depiction of Santa Muerte - it was so small because it was intended to hang from a necklace. I placed that small Santa Muerte medallion on a dresser and my first altar was born. You could also anchor an altar around a Santa Muerte prayer card, the kind that fits in a wallet, or even around an image downloaded to a cell phone or tablet.

It would be wonderful if you could keep your altar up all the time, but the Santa Muerte understands that this is not always possible. If you are in a situation where you can't erect a permanent Santa Muerte altar, you also have the option of creating a temporary Santa Muerte altar that you can put up and take down as required. Any altar can be a temporary altar, so long as you have a way of packing and storing all the pieces that go into it. You can build a temporary altar out of an old shoe box or cigar box, or use a larger plastic bin. Again, the altar should be shown some respect even when stored away and out of view - which is to say that you should not store it in an area of your home cluttered with junk, rather it should be stored with other items that you consider valuable and worth preserving.

There are lots of Santa Muerte altars in the world, from the tiny to the humongous, from the basic to the lavish. Just as each relationship with Santa Muerte is unique and special, so too is each altar that is erected in her name. You should use your altar as an opportunity to express yourself and your creativity. So long as the altar is constructed with the intent of showing your devotion to Santa Muerte, then your altar will be constructed correctly.

How to Build an Astral Santa Muerte Altar

When you can't build a physical altar to Santa Muerte, even a covert altar, you have the option of relying on an astral altar, which is an altar that exists within your mind's eye. This is something that I have also referred to as "the altar in one's heart". While the idea of visualizing Santa Muerte for the purposes of devotion is not a new idea, the term "astral altar" is one that I have not heard anywhere else in regard to Santa Muerte, so I have chosen to coin it here for our purposes.

Remember that the only requirement of a Santa Muerte altar is a depiction or representation of death - and any image that you can conjure in your mind is just as valid and powerful as any image you can find in the real world. Part of the reason altars are erected in the real world is to give our conscious minds something to focus on when we pray, petition, or make offerings to Santa Muerte. If you're able to focus on an image of the Santa Muerte in your mind, however, then you have everything you need for a Santa Muerte altar that you can take anywhere and that never needs to be dusted.

Similar to building a physical Santa Muerte altar, any depiction or representation of death will suffice as the foundation for an astral altar. This means that you can hold a literal representation of Santa Muerte in your mind's eye, or, if that is too difficult, you can try visualizing a more basic representation like a skull or vase of dead flowers. I encourage you to try visualizing a variety of different death related images until you find one that you can comfortably hold in your mind's eye. It would also be helpful to constantly review images of symbols associated with Santa Muerte in order to give your mind more and more material to draw inspiration from.

You may find that you have one type of image that you enjoy visualizing more than others, and you may find that the images you visualize will change depending on factors like your mood or the purpose of a magick petition. For example, if you wanted to offer a prayer of thanks for help in a matter of love, then you could visualize an astral altar anchored by the Santa Muerte dressed in red, as red is associated with matters of love, or you could visualize a vase of dead roses. If you wanted to petition the Santa Muerte for help with a legal matter, then you could visualize an astral altar anchored by the Santa Muerte dressed in green, as green is associated with the law, or you could visualize the scales of justice.

Using this astral altar is as simple as willing it into your mind's eye whenever you want to communicate with Santa Muerte, pray to her, or make an offering to her. Do not be discouraged if you lose focus while you work or pray. If you lose focus, simply regroup your thoughts and conjure the image into your mind's eye again.

If you are someone who absolutely cannot erect a physical altar, not even a covert altar, and if visualization is difficult for you, then you can create a type of astral altar substitute which I will call an altar of declared intent - essentially a type of astral altar that is prayed into existence rather than visualized. To be clear, this should only be considered an altar of last resort, because imagery, whether in the real world right in front of you, or visualized in your mind's eye, is a powerful tool for focusing your intent on the outcome you hope to achieve, and whenever you have access to a powerful tool of magick, then you should use it. This being said, to create an altar of declared intent, simply recite one time aloud or to yourself a declarative statement like;

"Santa Muerte, I acknowledge you,
I love you, and now I do approach you,"

Then perform whatever magickal work you have to perform as normal.

How to Make Offerings to Santa Muerte

To make an offering to Santa Muerte, you need to first decide why you are making the offering. Are you making the offering to ask for something specific in return? Or are you making the offering as thanks, with no expectations of reciprocation? Having a clear objective in your mind of why you want to make the offering will help guide you as you search for the appropriate offering to make. When you have an idea of why you want to make the offering, the next step is to select your offering.

Public Santa Muerte altars in Mexico are regularly adorned with offerings that include seven-day candles, bottles of tequila, cigarettes, candy bars, incense, and cash. The fact is, however, that practically anything can serve as an offering, so long as it is offered with the intent that it be a gift for Santa Muerte.

What I tell people is that the offerings you choose to give to Santa Muerte should be items that you yourself would like to receive as a gift. How would you feel if somebody gave you a pack of cigarettes or a candy bar? Are you the type that would instead prefer a fresh flower or a ripe piece of fruit? The reason we give offerings that we ourselves would like to receive is because part of the act of making the offering is the act of making a sacrifice. It makes a stronger statement to Santa Muerte when we give her something that we just as easily could have kept for ourselves, but instead decided to sacrifice so that she could receive it.

In keeping with offerings that you yourself would like to receive, there is also no obligation to offer items just because other devotees are offering them. For example, if you don't smoke or drink, then you should feel no obligation to offer cigarettes or alcohol to Santa Muerte.

Providing offerings that you yourself would like to receive will also ensure that you don't clutter your altar with things that have no other place. How would you feel, for example, if on your birthday you were given a gift with a card that read, "Here you go, I was just going to throw this out anyway." Would you appreciate the thought and effort that went into the gift? It is, after all, the thought that counts. Your altar is not a place to stack items that have no other place in your home, the altar should be treated with respect and the offerings should be made with real thought behind them. This is because, when it comes time to petition Santa Muerte for something you need or want, you would probably like for Santa Muerte to put thought and effort into helping you, rather than just tossing you the magickal scraps.

Placing an offering at a physical altar is pretty straightforward - you need only to set it down at your altar with the intent in your heart of giving it to Santa Muerte. When I place an offering at a physical altar, I like to place the offering, then kiss my hand and touch the depiction of Santa Muerte, followed by a simple prayer such as, "Santa Muerte, I make this offering for you." The process will be a little different if you're working with a temporary altar that is stored away when not in use, or an astral altar, which exists entirely in your mind's eye.

In the case of a temporary altar that is not currently on display, an offering can be made by placing the offering in the area where you store the rest of your Santa Muerte altar. For example, if you store your altar in a shoebox when not in use, then you could place your offering into the shoebox so that, in effect, it becomes part of your altar. The offering would then be displayed with the rest of your altar pieces when the altar was erected, and placed respectfully back into the storage container when the altar was put away. Again, a simple prayer can be recited as you place the offering, such as, "Santa Muerte, I make this offering for you."

In the case of an astral altar, an offering can be made by holding the offering in your hands, or placing the offering on a surface in front of you, and visualizing your astral altar in your mind's eye. You can then recite a simple prayer of offering, like "Santa Muerte, I make this offering for you," and then allow the offering to rest in a place of respect.

If you have no access to a physical altar and are unable to visualize an astral altar in your mind's eye, you may still make a successful offering by intending that an item be offered to Santa Muerte. This can be done by holding the offering in your hands, or placing it on a surface in front of you, and praying, "Santa Muerte, I make this offering for you," and then leaving the item in a place of respect. This is essentially the same as leaving an offering at an altar of declared intent, which was a concept discussed in the previous chapter.

In addition, offerings may be made to Santa Muerte by going to a place associated with death and leaving the offerings there. To do this, first take your offering to a place where the energy of death is strong, like a cemetary, graveyard, a hospital with an emergency room, a crossroads, or a bare tree - a tree whose leaves have all died and fallen off. Next, hold the offering in your hands and recite a simple prayer of offering, again like, "Santa Muerte, I make this offering for you", then leave the offering somewhere on the grounds of that place. If you leave the offering outside in nature, considerations should be made so the offering would not be mistaken for common litter, like offering a piece of fruit or a flower, instead of a candy in a wrapper.

Above all, remember that it is not where you make the offering that counts, but your intent of giving it to Santa Muerte. So long as you intend for the Santa

Muerte to receive the offering, then the offering will have been made successfully.

Frequency of Offerings to Santa Muerte

Offerings should be made to Santa Muerte whenever you ask her to grant you a favor, or as often as you are able. The offerings do not always need to be big offerings, but remember that a Santa Muerte devotee is one who acknowledges Santa Muerte. Regular offerings show the Santa Muerte that she holds a place in your heart, and that you are constantly acknowledging her.

The frequency of offerings will largely depend on your ability to make the offerings. Since you don't need an altar to make offerings, and since prayers can be a form of offering, there is no reason why an offering can't be made at least weekly, if not daily. Even if you have no money to buy an offering, you can still set aside five minutes of your day to dedicate a prayer or series of prayers to Holy Death.

Remember that the power of Santa Muerte comes from the relationship that you form with her. If you have convinced yourself that offerings are impossible, even simple offerings of prayers, then I personally do not see your relationship with Santa Muerte growing very strong.

When to Remove Offerings from an Altar

Beginning devotees often ask me how they know when to remove an offering from a Santa Muerte altar.

If the offering is organic, like an apple or flower, then it should be removed when it begins to show signs of going old or wilting. The only items on the altar that should appear dead are the depictions or representations of death that are the anchor of the altar. The offerings are separate from the depictions of death and should be kept in a state that you yourself would like to receive. Would you like to receive a brown apple or a wilting flower? If not, then they should be removed from the altar before they go bad.

As for other offering items that won't go bad or that may last a long time, like bottles of alcohol, cigarettes, or candy bars, these should be removed when you yourself begin to get bored of seeing them on your altar. If you are getting bored of seeing an offering item on your altar, then chances are good that the Santa Muerte is getting bored of seeing it as well, and it would be wise to rotate the item off the altar.

When it comes to how to dispose of offerings rotated off an altar, you may follow the instructions outlined in the chapter "How to Dispose of Magick Trash", which is shared a little later in this book.

How to Petition
the Santa Muerte

For Santa Muerte devotees, a petition is a
request. Anyone can request anything they want from
the Santa Muerte, but those who work on building the
strongest relationships are often those who have the
best results. It is not unheard of for Santa Muerte to
grant miracles for non-devotees with no history of a
relationship with her, which is why many in Mexico refer
to Santa Muerte as the Saint of Last Resorts - the one
who can be petitioned when gods and other spiritual
forces fail to offer results. If I had to guess, I would say
this was a tactic by Santa Muerte to show her power to
the world, as many non-devotees who are granted

miracles tend to become devotees once they see that Santa Muerte listened when all others did not.

The Santa Muerte is all around us, and nothing more is needed to petition the Santa Muerte than your own intent and your ability to articulate what it is that you want. On my website, SantaMuerteMagick.com, I offer full rituals that often involve colored candles, herbs, and special prayers, but these are not the only way that petitions can be made.

One of the hardest things for humans to do is focus in on exactly what it is that they want. If we do not know what we want, how can we expect Santa Muerte to deliver? This is why the petitions on my site include so many corresponding factors, like colors, herbs, and prayers - to help us focus in on what we want so we can make our intent absolutely clear when we offer the petition to Santa Muerte.

Remember that the power of Santa Muerte does not come from any physical item or string of rhyming words, it comes from our relationship with her. If you want to petition the Santa Muerte, you are free to use any of the rituals on my site, or you can simply close your eyes and pray something like, "Santa Muerte, please bring X into my life," or "Santa Muerte, please bless me with X". These are both examples of simple petition requests that you can recite. So long as your intent is made clear, then your petition can be delivered.

The reason why the petitions shared on my website are more elaborate than a simple prayer is because part of the ritual process is an offering of time and effort. By taking the time to gather the ritual supplies, and then taking the time to conduct the entire ritual, we show the Santa Muerte that we are serious about our intent and that we are serious about our devotion to her. Not everybody has the means to perform an entire ritual complete with burning candles and herbal offerings, and the Santa Muerte will not fault you if all you are able to do is offer a simple prayer for a petition, but I have found that people who are lazy about performing magick generally receive lazy results.

In other words, are you offering a simple prayer for a petition because it is all you can offer? Or are you offering a simple prayer because you don't want to go out and buy the necessary herbs or candles? Are you putting all the effort you can into your petition? Or are you taking the easy way out and looking for a quick fix? These are answers you do not have to justify to anybody but yourself, and you will know in your heart of hearts whether or not your effort is true.

What follows is a simple petition outline you can use to build your own petition rituals. It is intended for when you are in a best case scenario - meaning when you can afford the ritual tools and have access to them, and when you have a place where you can make the petition. In the next chapter, titled "Santa Muerte Petition Rituals", is a collection of magick petition rituals that are included as an example of what is possible by implementing the outline that follows.

Step 1 - Define the intent

Why are you petitioning the Santa Muerte? What exactly is it that you want? Who is the target of this petition; yourself or someone else? You should be able to articulate your intent in a single sentence. For example, "I want to deliver healing energy to person X", or, "I want person X and person Y to divorce", or "I want to attract more clients to my business."

Step 2 - Write or Find a Prayer

Whether you write a prayer of your own or find a prayer written by somebody else, there are a few pieces of advice that I would offer. First is that the prayer does not have to be very long - I find that prayers between four and 10 lines are the perfect length for a petition ritual. Next is to ensure that the prayer clearly embodies your intent, the intent you settled on in Step 1. The prayer should also invoke the name of Santa Muerte, so there is no confusion about who you are petitioning and who the prayer is intended for. Finally, I find prayers that rhyme are both easier to remember and more helpful for entering into a magickal state of mind - but this is a personal preference.

Step 3 - Select a Candle

Many of the petition rituals I share on my website feature a candle color-coded to the intent of the petition - red candles for love, gold candles for business, et cetera (see the chapter titled "Santa Muerte Color Correspondences" for more). The candle serves to illuminate your intent and to ensure that Santa Muerte will see your efforts. I also like candles because they offer a clear way to tell how long the petition should remain at your altar - which is until the candle burns to completion. In the event that you can't color code your candle to match your intent, a white candle may be substituted. Since the purpose of the candle is illumination, a wax candle is not necessarily required, and an electronic LED candle will work just fine. If using an LED candle, then leave the candle on for three to seven days, depending on how much power and effort you wish to commit to the petition. Generally, the bigger the ask, the more power and effort you should incorporate into the petition.

Step 4 - Find A Target Link

A target link is something in your petition that clearly links your intent to the person or place you want to affect. If you want to send a curse or hex, or if you want to send healing energies and blessings, incorporating a target link will make your petition all the more focused. You have several options for target links.

One of the most basic is to get something physical from your target, like a lock of hair or nail clippings. If the target of your petition is someone very close to you, then this might be easy. A good substitution for locks of hair and nail clippings is a photo of the target. In the absence of any of these, you can research any identifying information about your target and write that information onto a piece of paper - like a date of birth, home address, phone number, email address, or even a job title. One or two good target links is all you need, but the more links you incorporate into your petition, the more focused the intent behind your petition will be. Don't go crazy trying to track down target links - the last thing you want is to be confused for a stalker.

It may be that the target of your petition is a place - such as a home you want to protect or a business you want to hurt. In this case, the target link may be a picture of the place, or a paper bearing the full address of the place. Something physical from the place could also be used, such as a pinch of dirt from the property, or the key to the property's front door.

If you're petitioning Santa Muerte for yourself, a target link as described above is not entirely necessary, because you will act as your own link as you perform the rest of the ritual. However, there is nothing wrong with adding more power to a petition ritual, and you are free to incorporate a target link back to yourself if you wish.

Step 5 - Gather The Appropriate Herbs

Herbs have a long history in magick, and I like to incorporate them into Santa Muerte petitions because they can be blended in different combinations to petition for different goals.

For example, ginger is associated with new adventures, and could be added to a blend of rose (for love) and lavender (for lust) to attract new sexual partners. Ginger may also be added to a blend of cinnamon (for abundance) and Irish Moss (for attracting customers to a business) to attract new business clients. There is an entire list of herbal correspondences included in this book which you can experiment with. I like to blend three or four herbs together (usually) in order to create a blend for a specific petition. There is no right or wrong way to blend herbs - the only person you need to satisfy with your blend is yourself. As long as your blend makes sense to you, then it will make sense to Santa Muerte.

If you don't already have a mortar and pestle, then this would be the time to procure a set. In addition to helping you hone in on your intent, grinding and mixing herbs in a mortar and pestle allows you to focus on your intent and pour even more effort into your petition.

Step 6 - Go To Your Altar

When you have completed the steps above, then you can go to your Santa Muerte altar and begin the petition ritual. Start by lighting the candle so you may work in its light, and recite the selected prayer.

When the candle is set aflame, you may prepare your target link. This could be gathering the hair or nail clippings, or writing the target's personal information on a piece of paper. When the target link is ready, place it beneath the candle, so the intent of your petition may weigh directly on your target. If the link cannot be placed under the candle, then place it next to the candle in the candle's light, so your intent may shine directly on your target. Recite again your selected prayer.

Next, combine approximately equal amounts of your herbal ingredients in your mortar and pestle and grind until the mix is well incorporated. If you are working with an expensive herb, like saffron, then add what you can spare. If you are working with a resin, then freeze the resin to make it brittle and easier to grind.

The goal should be to grind and mix the herbal ingredients so there's a little bit of each ingredient in every pinch. As you grind the ingredients, continue to recite your chosen prayer while focusing on the intent of the petition.

When the herbal mixture is ground and incorporated so that a bit of each herb would be present in every pinch, then slowly begin to sprinkle the mixture, pinch by pinch, around the outside base of your burning candle. Continue to recite your selected prayer, until all of the herbs from your blend are encircling the base of the candle.

At this point, you may recite the prayer one last time, before considering your part in the petition complete. Allow the candle to burn to completion.

Anything remaining from this petition may be disposed according to the suggestions in the chapter titled "How to Dispose of Magick Trash".

If you are using traditional candles with a true flame, then please extinguish the candle when you cannot supervise its burning, and re-light the candle when you can. Also, never fall asleep with a burning candle in your home, and always keep a fire extinguisher nearby. Devotion takes many forms, but burning down your home is simply not practical.

Notes on Substitutions and Omissions

The outline I have just provided is a great way to petition the Santa Muerte, but I understand that you may not have access to all the ritual pieces as I have detailed here. Remember that the power of Santa Muerte comes from your relationship with her, not from any specific tool. If you do not have access to a physical altar, try conjuring an astral altar in your mind's eye. If you don't know how to write a prayer that rhymes, then simply create a statement in sentence form that asks the Santa Muerte to deliver the miracle you seek. If you do not have access to herbs that you can grind, you can still sit before your candle and pray as you focus on your intent.

This being said, I always encourage devotees to make substitutions as a last resort, not a first resort. Santa Muerte magick is about devotion and commitment, and if your first instinct is to strip away all the effort to make the ritual "easier", then do not be surprised if Santa Muerte strips away her effort from fulfilling your request. It is one thing if you don't have access to candles because you're dirt poor, in prison, or living with Christians - it's another thing entirely if you're being cheap or lazy. With Santa Muerte, it truly is the thought and effort that counts. So long as you make an effort, then you will strengthen your relationship with Santa Muerte and be far more likely to experience her blessings.

Santa Muerte Petition Rituals

Included here for your study are a few Santa Muerte petition rituals, based on the outline just presented in the previous chapter, "How to Petition the Santa Muerte". These petitions are offered so you can see how the outline previously provided can be implemented in a practical sense. For more petition ritual inspiration, please visit my website, SantaMuerteMagick.com.

Home Protection Santa Muerte Magick Petition

Step 1 - Define the Intent

The intent of this petition is to protect the home and all who live there from harm, misfortune, psychic attack, and hexes.

Step 2 - Write or Find a Magick Prayer

Here is an original prayer you can use as is or adapt:

"Santa Muerte in your white cloak,
protector of hearth and home,
in this place, love and abundance roam.
Family and friends, visitors and guests,
within these walls, may we face no threats.
Protect us from disasters and attackers,
from thieves, curse senders, and hex casters.
In the name of Holy Saint Death, amen."

Step 3 - Select a Candle

The candle color recommended for this petition is white, as white is associated with peace and calm.

Step 4 - Find a Target Link

Since the target of this petition is your home, your target link could be a picture of the home or a paper containing the home address. A copy of your lease agreement or mortgage statement would also work. Also gather all the names and dates of birth for everyone who lives in the home, to write on the picture or paper.

Step 5 - Gather the Appropriate Herbs

Basil - a strong protection herb against spiritual and physical harm.
Blessed Thistle - for home protection against thieves and unwanted visitors.
Fennel Seed - against negativity, curses, and to ward off bad luck.
Oregano - for tranquility, good luck, and protection.

Although not an herb, you may also incorporate into this blend a pinch or two of dirt from the target property you want to protect.

Step 6 - Go to Your Altar

Light the white candle so you may work in its light, and recite the selected magick prayer.

Take the target link you have chosen for this petition, and write on it all the names and dates of birth for everyone who lives in the home full-time. Place this target link under or next to the candle, and again recite the selected prayer.

Next, grind approximately equal parts of the basil, blessed thistle, fennel seed, and oregano with your mortar and pestle. If incorporating a pinch or two of dirt from the home to be protected, it may be added to the blend at this point. Continue to recite the selected magick prayer as you focus on your intent of protecting your home and those who live there from harm and misfortune. Be careful of breathing in the dust of the herbs as you grind, as it may cause irritation.

When the herbs have been ground to the point that a bit of each herb would be present in every pinch, then slowly begin to spread this herbal mixture, pinch by pinch, around the outside base of your candle. Continue to recite the magick prayer as you spread the herbs, until the entire herbal mixture has been distributed around the base of the candle.

Recite again the magick prayer, and allow the candle to burn at your altar until completion. If using an LED candle, then the candle should remain on your altar for three to seven days. Once complete, you may dispose of anything remaining from this petition using the suggestions in the chapter "How to Dispose of Magick Trash."

Steady Work Santa Muerte Magick Petition

Step 1 - Define the Intent

The intent of this petition is to secure steady work as an employee, contractor, small business owner, side hustler, etc.

Step 2 - Write or Find a Magick Prayer

Here is an original prayer you can use as is or adapt:

"Santa Muerte cloaked in gold,
Bring in work to have and hold.
Honest profit, payments clear,

always keep employers near.
Patron, Oh Saint Holy Death,
Put concerns of work to rest.
In your name, amen."

Step 3 - Select a Candle

The candle color recommended for this petition is gold, as gold is associated with success in work and business.

Step 4 - Find a Target Link

Since this petition is for steady work, the target link should be associated with the business of the target. A picture of the target in work uniform, or a picture of the business where the target works will work well. As would a business card or resume of the target. If you alone are the target, then no additional target link is necessary, but you may still incorporate a lock of your own hair, a photo of yourself, or something related to you and your business, if you feel it would help focus your intent and add power to the petition.

Step 5 - Gather the Appropriate Herbs

Basil - to dispel negativity / curses which may be standing in the way of steady work. Also encourages money, wealth, success, and prosperity.

Irish Moss - to ensure a steady flow of cash, to bring customers in business.

Patchouli - to draw money in general.

Step 6 - Go to Your Altar

Light the gold candle so you may work in its light, and recite the selected magick prayer.

Take the target link you have chosen for this petition, place this target link under or next to the candle, and again recite the selected prayer.

Next, grind approximately equal parts of the basil, Irish Moss, and patchouli, with your mortar and pestle. Continue to recite the selected magick prayer as you focus on your intent of bringing a steady flow of work into the target's life. Be careful of breathing in the dust of the herbs as you grind, as it may cause irritation.

When the herbs have been ground to the point that a bit of each herb would be present in every pinch, then slowly begin to spread this herbal mixture, pinch by pinch, around the outside base of your candle. Continue to recite the magick prayer as you spread the herbs, until the entire herbal mixture has been distributed around the base of the candle.

Recite again the magick prayer, and allow the candle to burn at your altar until completion. If using an LED candle, then the candle should remain on your altar for three to seven days. Once complete, you may dispose of anything remaining from this petition using the suggestions in the chapter "How to Dispose of Magick Trash."

Go Away Santa Muerte Magick Petition

Step 1 - Define the Intent

The intent of this petition is to get rid of a problem person from your life - for example, a bad boss, a bully, a bad neighbor, et cetera.

Step 2 - Write or Find a Magick Prayer

Here is an original prayer you can use as is or adapt:

"Holy Death, to you I pray,
Send this person far away.
This person who brings me strife,
Remove them quick, from my life.
Where they go, I do not care,
Just be anywhere but here.
Amen."

Step 3 - Select a Candle

The candle color recommended for this petition is black, as black is associated with repelling negative forces.

Step 4 - Find a Target Link

Since this petition is to send someone out of your life, the target link should be associated with the person you want to send away. A picture of the target can be used, or the person's identifying information on a piece of paper.

Step 5 - Gather the Appropriate Herbs

Basil - to dispel negativity and repel hostile forces.
Cayenne Pepper - to light a fire under your target's ass, to get them moving on.
Wormwood - for sending away, to evict your target from your life..

Step 6 - Go to Your Altar

Light the black candle so you may work in its light, and recite the selected magick prayer.

Take the target link you have chosen for this petition, place this target link under or next to the candle, and again recite the selected prayer.

Next, grind approximately equal parts of the basil, cayenne pepper, and wormwood, with your mortar and pestle. Continue to recite the selected magick prayer as you focus on your intent of sending your target out of your life. Be careful of breathing in the dust of the herbs as you grind, as it may cause irritation.

When the herbs have been ground to the point that a bit of each herb would be present in every pinch, then slowly begin to spread this herbal mixture, pinch by pinch, around the outside base of your candle. Continue to recite the magick prayer as you spread the herbs, until the entire herbal mixture has been distributed around the base of the candle.

Recite again the magick prayer, and allow the candle to burn at your altar until completion. If using an LED candle, then the candle should remain on your altar for three to seven days. Once complete, you may dispose of anything remaining from this petition using the suggestions in the chapter "How to Dispose of Magick Trash."

Lover Come to Me Santa Muerte Magick Petition

Step 1 - Define the Intent

The intent of this petition is to draw a long lasting lover into your life.

Step 2 - Write or Find a Magick Prayer

Here is an original prayer you can use as is or adapt:

"Skeleton Saint, dressed in red,
Bring a lover to my bed.
Destroy what keeps the love away,
Long lasting love, come my way.
Let times be good, sex be hot,
Bring love and sex, lots and lots.
In your name, amen."

Step 3 - Select a Candle

The candle color recommended for this petition is red, as red is associated with all matters of love and sex.

Step 4 - Find a Target Link

Since this petition is to attract a lover into your life, you alone are the target, and no additional target link is necessary, but you may still incorporate a lock of your own hair, a photo of yourself, or a paper with your name and date of birth, if you feel it would help focus your intent and add power to your petition.

Step 5 - Gather the Appropriate Herbs

Rose - for attracting a lasting love.
Rosemary - also for attracting a lasting love.
Catnip - to trigger an attraction.

Step 6 - Go to Your Altar

Light the red candle so you may work in its light, and recite the selected magick prayer.

If you have elected to create a target link for yourself, place this target link under or next to the candle, and again recite the selected prayer.

Next, grind approximately equal parts of the rose, lavender, and ginger, with your mortar and pestle. Continue to recite the selected magick prayer as you focus on your intent of sending your target out of your life. Be careful of breathing in the dust of the herbs as you grind, as it may cause irritation.

When the herbs have been ground to the point that a bit of each herb would be present in every pinch, then slowly begin to spread this herbal mixture, pinch by pinch, around the outside base of your candle. Continue to recite the magick prayer as you spread the herbs, until the entire herbal mixture has been distributed around the base of the candle.

Recite again the magick prayer, and allow the candle to burn at your altar until completion. If using an LED candle, then the candle should remain on your altar for three to seven days. Once complete, you may dispose of anything remaining from this petition using the suggestions in the chapter "How to Dispose of Magick Trash."

Health and Healing Santa Muerte Magick Petition

Step 1 - Define the Intent

The intent of this petition is to send healing energy to one physically or emotionally unwell. Remember; magick is a tool, not a cure. Always use magick in conjunction with modern medicine.

Step 2 - Write or Find a Magick Prayer

Here is an original prayer you can use as is or adapt:

"Holy Death, merciful saint,
Please relieve the aches and pains.
Health of body, and of mind,
Send your power in quick time.
Amen."

Step 3 - Select a Candle

The candle color recommended for this petition is yellow, as yellow is associated with health and healing.

Step 4 - Find a Target Link

Your target link should relate to the person you would like the Santa Muerte to heal. A photo of the person, or the person's identifying information on a piece of paper, would make an acceptable target link.

Step 5 - Gather the Appropriate Herbs

Basil - to dispel negativity which may be lending itself to ill health.

Cloves - to encourage the healing of physical ailments, especially physical pain.

Lavender - to encourage the healing of mental / emotional pain.

Step 6 - Go to Your Altar

Light the yellow candle so you may work in its light, and recite the selected magick prayer.

Take the target link you have chosen for this petition, place this target link under or next to the candle, and again recite the selected prayer.

Next, grind approximately equal parts of the basil, cloves, and lavender, with your mortar and pestle. Continue to recite the selected magick prayer as you focus on your intent of delivering healing energies to your target. Be careful of breathing in the dust of the herbs as you grind, as it may cause irritation.

When the herbs have been ground to the point that a bit of each herb would be present in every pinch, then slowly begin to spread this herbal mixture, pinch by pinch, around the outside base of your candle.

Continue to recite the magick prayer as you spread the herbs, until the entire herbal mixture has been distributed around the base of the candle.

Recite again the magick prayer, and allow the candle to burn at your altar until completion. If using an LED candle, then the candle should remain on your altar for three to seven days. Once complete, you may dispose of anything remaining from this petition using the suggestions in the chapter "How to Dispose of Magick Trash."

Intuition and Psychic Dreams
Santa Muerte Magick Petition

Step 1 - Define the Intent

The intent of this petition is to increase psychic intuition, especially psychic dreams.

Step 2 - Write or Find a Magick Prayer

Here is an original prayer you can use as is or adapt:

"Santa Muerte, show to me,
Psychic visions in my dreams.
Signs and symbols all around,
Show to me the future now.
Let my third eye open bright,
And bless me with second sight.
Amen."

Step 3 - Select a Candle

The candle color recommended for this petition is purple, as purple is associated with psychic abilities and intuition.

Step 4 - Find a Target Link

Since this petition is to increase your own psychic powers and intuition, you alone are the target, and no additional target link is necessary, but you may still incorporate a lock of your own hair, a photo of yourself, or a paper with your name and date of birth, if you feel it would help you focus your intent and add power to your petition.

Step 5 - Gather the Appropriate Herbs

Anise - to increase psychic abilities.

Bay Leaf - to stimulate psychic powers.

Jasmine - for accuracy in divination and the interpretation of signs / symbols.

Step 6 - Go to Your Altar

Light the purple candle so you may work in its light, and recite the selected magick prayer.

If you have elected to create a target link for yourself, place this target link under or next to the candle, and again recite the selected prayer.

Next, grind approximately equal parts of the anise, bay leaf, and jasmine, with your mortar and pestle. Continue to recite the selected magick prayer as you focus on your intent of receiving psychic dreams and boosting your intuition. Be careful of breathing in the dust of the herbs as you grind, as it may cause irritation.

When the herbs have been ground to the point that a bit of each herb would be present in every pinch, then slowly begin to spread this herbal mixture, pinch by pinch, around the outside base of your candle. Continue to recite the magick prayer as you spread the herbs, until the entire herbal mixture has been distributed around the base of the candle.

Recite again the magick prayer, and allow the candle to burn at your altar until completion. If using an LED candle, then the candle should remain on your altar for three to seven days. Once complete, you may dispose of anything remaining from this petition using the suggestions in the chapter "How to Dispose of Magick Trash."

How to Make a Contract with Santa Muerte

A contract is a bargain with Santa Muerte for her to grant one specific miracle in exchange for you to perform one specific deed in return. The difference between a petition and a contract is that when you make a petition, you are making an offering at the time of the request, where a contract reserves the offering until the Santa Muerte has delivered.

The beauty of the contract is that your obligation to Santa Muerte does not come due unless you get what you want. This is good if you are not a devotee because it allows you to make the request without feeling like you owe anything. You will know if the Santa Muerte accepted your offer because you will have what you asked for. Once you have what you asked for, your end of the bargain will come due, and you should work to accomplish whatever it was that you promised within a reasonable amount of time.

To make the contract with Santa Muerte, you need only document what it is that you want and what it is that you are willing to do in return if you get it. This can be as simple as writing on a piece of paper or typing into a digital document, "Santa Muerte, if you grant me the miracle of ABC, then I will perform the deed of XYZ." Mark the document with your full name and the date of creation.

If for some reason you change your mind after making the offer to Santa Muerte, you can revoke your offer if she has not yet fulfilled your request. No harm, no foul. This is accomplished by destroying the documentation of your contract. If she has already fulfilled your request and you are unable or unwilling to keep up with your end of the bargain, then you run the risk of your favor or miracle turning sour.

In regard to what you should offer in return for a miracle or favor granted by Santa Muerte, that's entirely up to you, but I find that big requests require big deeds, and small requests can be satisfied with small deeds.

What is big and what is small? That's all relative to you and your life. Asking for a child may be a big or small request, depending on how difficult it is for you to conceive. Asking for a new job or financial opportunity may be a big or small request, depending on how dire your financial situation.

What you offer in return will also be relative to your life. If you promise to donate cash to a Santa Muerte altar or other Santa Muerte related project, is $100 a lot of money to you, or is it a little? If you promise to donate your time to a charity that brings comfort to the dying, does 100 hours seem like a lot of time, or a little? If you promise to recite prayers of devotion to Santa Muerte, does 100 consecutive days of prayer seem like a lot, or does it seem like a little? In my experience, your conscience will know whether you are making a suitable promise or coming up short. If you get the nagging feeling that you're coming up short, then consider increasing what it is that you will promise in return.

This being said, you should never promise more than you are able to deliver. Just as your conscience will know whether you're offering too little or just enough, your conscience will also know whether you are actually capable of delivering. If you are simply not emotionally strong enough to volunteer at a place that brings comfort to the dying, then you should not make the promise in the first place.

Once you make the contract, there is the possibility that Santa Muerte will not deliver. I recommend you give the Santa Muerte three months to fulfill your request. If the request is not fulfilled by the end of three months, then you can consider the contract rejected by Santa Muerte. If this happens, you can adjust the terms of the contract - perhaps ask for something slightly different and possibly increase what you were offering in return - or destroy the original contract and walk away. If the Santa Muerte did not provide what you were asking for, then you do not owe anything in return.

What Happens If You Break a Promise with Santa Muerte?

One type of email I get through my website is from people who have broken promises to Santa Muerte and who want to know if they will be okay and whether or not they can come back to Santa Muerte.

Will you be okay if you break a promise? I don't know, but most likely. The Santa Muerte is a force so powerful that she does not need to be petty.

Can you come back to Santa Muerte? Remember, the Santa Muerte accepts us all, because she will one day come for us all. In this sense, you never left.

The Santa Muerte does not punish or seek retribution - she does not need to because she has already won, because you are already a mortal who will one day die. Like a parent who is made to feel unappreciated and unacknowledged, the Santa Muerte may not stop loving you, but she may choose to stop taking an active role in your life. Personally, if I ever broke a promise to Santa Muerte, I would not feel like I was in danger of punishment, I would feel more like I was in danger of being ignored and being overlooked when she handed out her blessings.

On the bright side, the relationship between Santa Muerte and devotee is just that - a relationship. Like all relationships connected by true love, it is not impossible for one to come back from a broken promise, the effort just has to be made. In other words, if you feel you have broken a promise to Santa Muerte, then you can work on healing the relationship by making promises and keeping them. This could be promising to spend more time with Santa Muerte by acknowledging her more throughout your day. It could also be promising to make regular offerings, and then making sure that the offerings get made. You may stumble, as humans often do stumble, but what matters most is what's in your heart and the continued effort that you make to keep your relationship strong.

When Petitions or Contracts Go Unanswered

There are no guarantees when working with Santa Muerte - except the one, and that is your own death. I do not know why Santa Muerte chooses to grant some petitions but not others. The petitions she chooses to grant are her prerogative, as she is not a force which can be commanded. Even those of us with strong relationships with Santa Muerte will have petitions that go unanswered. This being said, you should never not ask for something that you want or need. When we make the effort and ask, there is a chance we can get what we asked for, and that chance gets greater as our relationship with Santa Muerte gets stronger. If we make no effort to ask at all, we can't fault the Santa Muerte for overlooking us.

Whether it's a petition or a contract, it can be frustrating when Santa Muerte fails to grant us what we're looking for. Fortunately, we do have some options when this happens.

I generally advise anyone asking the Santa Muerte for her help in a matter to give it about three months before considering the petition or contract unfulfilled. If three months have passed with no positive result, then I would assess how the petition or contract was made, adjust, and try again. If your petition was made through simple prayer, then I would try the entire process again, but this time add a physical offering of some kind. If the petition was made with a physical offering, I would try the entire process again with a bigger offering, or with more time invested in the performance of the petition ritual. Likewise, if a contract goes three months with no answer, then I would destroy the original contract, and make a new contract that increases what you are promising to give in return.

Next, if another three months pass with no progress, I would consider changing what it is that I was asking for. For example, if I was looking for the love of a specific person, and two petitions or contracts went unanswered, I would adjust my request to ask for a love in general. If I was looking to get a specific job with a specific company, and two petitions or contracts went unanswered, I would adjust my request to be open to employment at any company.

After making the third request, if the Santa Muerte still does not grant the petition, then I would take the hint and let the matter rest for at least three months, before coming back to try again, if at all. The Christians have a saying, "Thank god for unanswered prayers." Again, I do not know why the Santa Muerte grants some petitions and not others, but in my experience an unanswered petition is often a doorway to a new blessing that I simply wasn't expecting.

Back when I was a freelance writer creating content for businesses, I petitioned the Santa Muerte to send me clients. Instead of getting more and more writing clients, I found myself getting more and more readers to my Santa Muerte website. I was petitioning Santa Muerte to make me a successful writer, but it never crossed my mind to petition the Santa Muerte to make me *her* writer. In refusing to grant my early business petitions, the Santa Muerte has led me down a path to be a writer for her and her devotees. Looking back, knowing what I know now, I'm very glad those earlier petitions were ignored.

Finally, do not forget that devotion to Santa Muerte is a devotion to your best possible death, whatever that may be for you. In this regard, if you ask for something that might take you away from a santa muerte, away from a good death, then it is reasonable to expect the Santa Muerte to ignore your petition in order to keep you on the path that will lead you to the best possible death you can experience.

Do I Have to Pray
to Santa Muerte Forever
If I Ask Her for Something?

No.

In the long run, the Santa Muerte has already won. The Santa Muerte will one day cut the thread of your life, and there's nothing you can do to stop it. If you choose to ask the Santa Muerte for a miracle once or twice, there's nothing that says you must devote yourself to her for the rest of your life.

Remember, however, that the power of Santa Muerte comes from the relationship you build with her. If all you do is ask of the Santa Muerte, take her blessings without offering anything in return, then it is not likely she will take an active role in your life until it is time for your death. The Santa Muerte will not forsake you - as she will still come for you in the end - but she may not be encouraged to keep granting you blessings and miracles if all you do is take, take, take, without making any effort to return the favor in the long run.

If you do intend to ask Santa Muerte for a miracle, but you are not sure if you want to devote yourself to Santa Muerte by acknowledging her on a regular basis, then I would recommend that you make a contract with Santa Muerte. When you make a contract, you are asking for one specific favor granted by Santa Muerte, in exchange for one specific deed performed by you. As explained in the chapter "How to Make a Contract with Santa Muerte", if the Santa Muerte grants your favor through contract, and you perform the deed that you promised to perform, then your obligation to Santa Muerte will be met, and you can go back to your regular life without having to declare yourself a full time devotee of Santa Muerte, and without owing anything else to Holy Death.

How to Build the Strongest Relationship Possible with Santa Muerte

The power of the Santa Muerte comes from the relationship you have with her. The stronger your relationship, the more you will find that your petitions / contracts are answered and that the Santa Muerte smiles on your life. Once you choose to become a devotee, which is to acknowledge death on a regular basis, the question becomes, how do you build the strongest relationship possible with Santa Muerte?

The trick to building the strongest relationship possible with Santa Muerte is to recognize that death is always with you, and to acknowledge her presence whenever you can. You don't have to be flamboyantly evangelical, the Santa Muerte appreciates every act of devotion which a devotee is able to provide.

When you wake in the morning, you can offer a prayer of thanks to Santa Muerte for allowing you to greet one more day:

"Santa Muerte, thank you for giving me one more day."

When you sit down to eat a meal, you can offer a prayer of thanks to Santa Muerte for allowing you to receive the meal:

"Santa Muerte, thank you for this meal I am about to receive."

When you go for a walk in the morning, or commute to work, you can offer an invitation for Santa Muerte to join you on your journey:

"Santa Muerte, I invite you on this journey with me."

Before going to bed in the evening, you can offer a prayer of thanks for the day you were allowed to live, and for a blessing as you sleep:

"Santa Muerte, thank you for the day I had, and bless me as I go to sleep."

In addition to offering prayers to Santa Muerte throughout the day, you can also keep an eye out for little offerings that you can make. When you make an offering to Santa Muerte without asking for anything in return, then no offering is too small, and it truly is the thought that counts. It could be a flower picked on your daily walk, a small chocolate from the corner market, or a stick of incense from your local new age shop. Just as you might surprise someone you love with a small gift or trinket for no reason, you can also surprise the Santa Muerte to constantly reinforce the fact that you acknowledge her and appreciate her active presence in your life.

How to Dispose of Magick Trash

During the practice of Santa Muerte magick, you may find yourself in the position of having items left over that need to be disposed. Perhaps it's the glass casing for a candle that has burned to completion, a mixture of herbs that was sprinkled around a candle, or a bottle of tequila you made as an offering.

Once a petition has been made, anything that is left over - unless you are keeping it to act as a magick charm - is essentially magick trash, and this chapter will discuss how to dispose of that magick trash in a safe and practical way. This advice can also be followed to deal with old offerings which you want to rotate off a Santa Muerte altar.

In the past, I would have recommended burning or burying items left over after magickal work, but no longer. In our modern age, and considering the number of devotees practicing in urban cities, burning or burying is not as prudent as it once was and is simply not necessary in a majority of cases.

Treating as Regular Trash

Is the item something that you would normally put in the garbage or recycling bin to be hauled to the dump? Then toss it in the appropriate garbage or recycling bin. Is it an item you would toss to the birds, like a piece of bread? Then toss it to the birds. Is it an item you would toss in your garden or compost bin to fertilize the soil, like fruit or old herbs? Then send it to the garden / compost bin.

Items which are treated as regular trash do not need to be magickally cleansed in any way, because if it is your intent to toss the item away as trash, then your intent will extend to the magick energy associated with the item. Tossing something away as regular trash, bird food, or compost, sends a very clear message that you are done with the item and no longer require any magick energy to be connected to the item.

It is only if you intend to reuse the item, or to give the item away for someone else to use, that you may consider it good practice to clarify your intent to preserve the item, but remove the energy you attached to it.

Reusing / Giving Away

It's an expensive world out there, and throwing away a perfectly good item just because it was used in a magickal petition or as an offering may not feel right to many modern Santa Muerte devotees. In the event an item is still good enough to be used and saved from the trash, you may decide to keep the item for future use, or to give the item away.

If the item was an offering to Santa Muerte, then it should not be kept for yourself. If the item is not treated as regular trash, then it should be given away for someone else to use. Remember that part of the act of making an offering is making a sacrifice, so if you keep the item for yourself, it would negate the act of the sacrifice.

If the item was a tool in a magickal petition, and if you decide to reuse the item or give it away, you can cleanse the item of the magickal energy you attached to it in the following way:

At your Santa Muerte altar, you can either anoint the item with a cleansing perfume or cologne, like Florida Water, OR you can pass the item through the smoke of a cleansing incense, such as sage or copal, OR you can sprinkle the item with a cleansing herb, like basil.

As you anoint the item, pass the item through smoke, OR sprinkle the item with an appropriate herb, visualize any magickal energy attached to the item rising from the item like steam evaporating into the air. As you visualize this, recite the following prayer over the item a total of three times:

"Santa Muerte, Holy Death,
let this energy now rest.
Make this item clean and pure,
to be made anew once more."

If you can wash the item with soap and water, then this should also be done, just to ensure the item is physically clean before any future use. You may now re-use the item or give it away as normal.

Final Notes

In the case of offerings left outside at places associated with death, like a cemetery or the grounds of a hospital, the item does not need to be retrieved and you can leave it to the elements, but considerations should be made so the item is not misinterpreted as common litter and so it will not harm the environment in which you place it. It would be better to leave a piece of fruit or a flower outside rather than a candy in a wrapper or a soda in a can.

In the case of cash offerings, you are free to spend any cash accumulated at your altar by reinvesting it back into the altar. Examples of reinvesting back into the altar include buying new altar pieces or artwork to display at your altar, or buying new offerings to make to Santa Muerte at the altar. You may also donate this cash to the poor. Reinvesting and donating to the poor are both common practices in Mexico where public altars can amass lots of cash in a matter of days.

Santa Muerte Color Correspondences

The Santa Muerte is often depicted wearing cloaks of different colors. These different colored cloaks represent different aspects of the Santa Muerte, rather than distinct individual entities. In other words, they are all the same Santa Muerte.

Technically, because all cloak colors represent the same energy, you may pray and petition to any aspect of Santa Muerte that you wish. The different colors are more for your benefit than for the Santa Muerte, as they can be useful when trying to focus your intent for one specific goal, which in turn may help to make your magick more powerful. In the petition rituals that I write, I generally introduce the color correspondence through the offering candle, and try to match the candle color to the intent of the petition. You may also introduce altar cloths of different colors and various accessories of different colors, like markers and burn plates. How you choose to incorporate the color correspondences are up to you, but they are as follows:

White: Believed by followers to be the most neutral energy to work with, the white Santa Muerte is called on to purify, cleanse, invite peace, and instill harmony. She is known to protect against accidents and misfortune.

Black: The most potent energy to work with, the black Santa Muerte can be called on both to send curses and break curses. Also associated with repelling negative energy.

Red: The Santa Muerte of love, passion, sex, and attraction. Lovers may pray to the red Santa Muerte for a healthy and long lasting relationship. Single people may pray to the red Santa Muerte for a spouse or casual lover, while people already in committed relationships may pray for the fidelity of their partner.

Pink: Having dominion over what you see in the mirror, this aspect of the Santa Muerte may be petitioned for matters relating to beauty and love of self.

Gold: If it's money and material success you want, it's the gold Santa Muerte you should turn to. Work with the gold Santa Muerte to attract money, business success, material wealth, and prosperity. It's common to see the gold Santa Muerte in markets and places of business.

Silver / Copper: For the kind of success hoped for by gamblers and card players. This is the aspect of Saint Death who you pray to when you need a stroke of luck, and before you head to the casino.

Green: The green aspect of the Santa Muerte is typically associated with justice and the legal profession, but it is also associated with fertility. The green Santa Muerte is a patron saint of attorneys and judges, but you may call on her for help in legal matters, when you want to avoid court / attention from law enforcement, or when you require justice but don't have the means to go to court or to pay for representation.

Green is the color of land, which itself represents legal jurisdictions (as in "the law of the land"), and personal property (which is at the center of many lawsuits). As a fertility symbol, the green Santa Muerte can be petitioned when you need something to grow and flourish, such as when you're trying to have a baby.

Blue: Wisdom and creativity are the energies most associated with the blue Santa Muerte. She is frequently revered by students, educators, academics, and artists. Work with the blue Santa Muerte for comprehension, understanding, and inspiration.

Purple: The color purple in Santa Muerte magick is associated with psychic abilities and intuition. Work with the purple aspect of the Santa Muerte when you want to divine the future, for increasing psychic abilities, for prophetic dreams and other forms of dream work, and for finding spiritual peace and harmony.

Yellow: The realm of health and healing is associated with the yellow Santa Muerte. A symbol of both physical and mental health, she is the patron saint of both healers and the sick, medical staff and their patients.

Transparent amber is often considered the color of addiction and rehabilitation.

Brown: The color of dirt, which fittingly represents the grave, brown is the aspect of Santa Muerte dealing in matters of the realm of the dead, necromancy, and spirits. She is who you should invoke and work with when attempting to communicate with or petition the dead. Remember to always go through the Santa Muerte before working with the dead, and to use divination to determine whether or not you have permission to proceed with your magickal work beyond the veil of the living. This is considered advanced work and should not be performed by novices.

Multi-Color: If you do some searching online for images and depictions of the Santa Muerte in various colors, you will no doubt come across rainbow and multi-colored Santa Muerte statues. The multi-colored cloak is just a way to receive the positive effects of each color without the need for several statues on a single altar. When you don't have the space or the funds for several different statues, or when you want to work with the Santa Muerte on different aspects of your life, a multi-colored statue offers a solution.

Santa Muerte Herb Correspondences

There are many ways to focus your magickal intent when petitioning the Santa Muerte, and herbs can be a great way to do that. Not everybody will have access to herbs, but if you do, you can use them to create magick powders or charms to focus the intent of your magick petition all the more. Remember; herbs in Santa Muerte magick are intended to be used as external tools - not consumed.

NOTE: Some of these herbs are actually resins. If you need to grind a resin, I recommend freezing the resin before your work, to make it more brittle and less likely to gum up your formula.

What follows are the herb correspondences that I use to create my own Santa Muerte petition rituals:

Agrimony - a powerful breaking and reflection herb against lies and slander. Also returns negative energy, hexes, and curses to those who send them. Acts as a defense shield.

Alfalfa - a powerful anti-hunger herb, alfalfa was often placed by the superstitious in cupboards and pantries to ensure they were always full. Said to attract prosperity and money, and to attract prosperity to gamblers when combined with other gambler related herbs.

Allspice - to attract surprise cash and treasure.

Anise - to increase psychic abilities and for psychic protection.

Basil - to dispel negativity and curses. Encourages money, wealth, success, and prosperity. To exorcise and repel hostile spirits; for protection and purification. To dispel confusion, fear, and weakness. Protection from evil in general.

Bay Leaf - a messenger herb, used to stimulate psychic powers, and return curses and hexes to senders.

Bergamot - for money, also attracts restful sleep so your money troubles don't keep you up at night.

Black Mustard Seed - to bring confusion and general discomfort to a target. To cause confusion for law enforcement, to trip up the law.

Black Pepper - to promote the breaking of bad habits.

Bladderwrack - for protection while traveling by water.

Boneset - to promote new opportunities, to open the road ahead and clear roadblocks that might stand in your way. "Abrecaminos" in Spanish, which literally translates to "Open Roads".

Calamus Root - to gain control over another person or situation. Calamus doesn't turn people into zombie-slaves, but it can ensure that your target sees you as positively confident, charming, and charismatic. This will make it much easier for you to get what you want or need from them.

Caraway Seeds - associated with fidelity. Known to keep away thieves, especially thieves of your lover's heart.

Catnip - to trigger an attraction.

Cayenne Pepper - To add heat and fire to a petition. May be directed as a physical heat to cause your target fever or pain, a spiritual heat to invade your target's dreams with fire and anger, or as an emotional heat to make your target angry, suspicious, and feeling like the walls are closing in. Can melt away desires if you want a target to leave you alone and move along. To light a fire under a target's ass and get them to take action. Can also be added to weight loss spells, to burn away calories and unwanted fat (always use magick in conjunction with traditional treatments / therapies).

Chamomile - for gambler's luck as it is often associated with attracting luck and money. Many traditions tell of gamblers washing their hands in chamomile tea before playing any games of chance. May be added to healing petitions to encourage healing of skin conditions and burns (always use magick in conjunction with traditional treatments / therapies).

Cinnamon - a prosperity herb, and a luxury in certain ancient societies, often incorporated to attract abundance, satisfaction, and fullness. Often carried by gamblers for luck, as it is associated with drawing in money. May be added to healing petitions to encourage healing of diabetes, blood, or circulation issues (always use magick in conjunction with traditional treatments / therapies).

Cloves - to attract friends and prevent gossip, for self confidence. May be added to healing petitions for conditions of the mouth, teeth, and gums, as well as to encourage healing of physical pain in general. Also associated in healing petitions with encouraging relief from cold and allergy symptoms. Always use magick in conjunction with traditional treatments / therapies.

Copal - known as a powerful spiritual protector and purifier, copal has a long history in Mexico for its connection to the dead, and it's considered one of the Santa Muerte's favorite incense aromas. Often used by devotees to represent the spiritual, magickal, and mystical nature of Santa Muerte.

Coriander - to keep a lover faithful.

Dragon's Blood - for warding off evil and bringing good luck.

Eucalyptus - for protection, and credited with working against snitches and informants.

Fennel Seed - against negativity, curses, and to ward off bad luck.

Feverfew - for protection while traveling by land.

Ginger - Draws adventure and new experiences. Promotes sensuality, sexuality, and personal confidence. Added to healing petitions to encourage healing of diabetes, blood / circulation issues, high cholesterol, and joint / bone pain (always use magick in conjunction with traditional treatment / therapies).

Hyssop - associated with cleansings and purification, well known for making ordinary spaces into holy spaces.

Irish Moss - to ensure a steady flow of cash, to bring customers in business.

Jalapeno Powder - another herb for adding heat and fire to a petition.

Jasmine - for accurate divination readings using tools like tarot cards or pendulums.

Lavender - for attracting sexual lust. Added to healing petitions to encourage healing of mental health issues and depression (always use magick in conjunction with traditional treatments / therapies).

Lemon Verbena - for causing strife and turmoil between two people (husband and wife, parent and child, boss and employee, etc.). To cause a divorce or breakup.

Licorice Root - to change the thoughts of another person, to push another person's mind in the direction you choose, to make your target more receptive to your ideas, to keep something on someone's mind.

Lucky Hand Root - for good luck while traveling and general protection.

Lungwort - for protection while traveling by air.

Mandrake Root - to cause physical pain, sickness, or disease. CAUTION - known to be poisonous, avoid skin contact and store in a secure place.

Motherwort - to attract self confidence and boost ego, for combatting self defeating attitudes.

Mugwort - for prophetic dreams.

Mustard - added to healing petitions to encourage the healing of cancer (always use magick in conjunction with traditional treatments / therapies).

Nettle - for strength of will, for help with handling emergencies.

Nutmeg - for gambler's luck, good fortune in games of chance and betting. Carried whole by gamblers in the past as a good luck charm.

Oregano - for tranquility, good luck, and protection. Added to healing petitions to encourage healing from foodborne illnesses and bacterial infections (always use magick in conjunction with traditional treatments / therapies).

Parsley - added to healing petitions to encourage healing of digestion issues (always use magick in conjunction with traditional treatments / therapies).

Patchouli - to draw money in general.

Peppermint - for focus, concentration, and alertness.

Poppy Seeds - to attract prosperity to the home, so you always have the money for the things you need. When added to a curse or hex petition, encourages mental confusion in your target, the kind of confusion that distracts and causes one to make poor decisions.

Red Clover - added to healing petitions to encourage healing of musculo conditions and muscle pain (always use magick in conjunction with traditional treatments / therapies).

Rose - for attracting a long lasting love. To devotees, also represents the softer, loving, and merciful side of the Santa Muerte.

Rosemary - Also known to attract a long lasting love. Also for memory and luck during exams. Added to healing petitions to encourage healing of brain disorders (always use magick in conjunction with traditional treatments / therapies).

Saffron - to promote sensuality, the pursuit of sexual pleasure.

Sage - for wisdom and mental strength. Also removes and repels negative energy / cleanses physical areas. Added to healing petitions to encourage healing of throat conditions (always use magick in conjunction with traditional treatments / therapies).

Sassafras - to bring good fortune in matters of money, and to help you stretch the money you do have.

Slippery Elm Bark - against lies and against gossip.

Sulfur - or "brimstone", to destroy a target's power over you. To rid your target from your life and your thoughts. CAUTION - known to be poisonous, avoid skin contact and store in a secure place.

Tansy - for causing nightmares. CAUTION - known to be poisonous, avoid skin contact and store in a secure place.

Blessed Thistle - for home protection against thieves and unwanted visitors.

Tobacco - to diminish a target's energy, vitality, power, and authority. For causing personal stagnation, as well as encouraging impotence in men. To devotees, can also represent the many vices of Santa Muerte, her down-to-Earth attitude, and live-for-the-moment spirit.

Turmeric - added to healing petitions to encourage healing of cancer, as well as conditions of the brain or head (always use magick in conjunction with traditional treatments / therapies).

Wheat Flour - to represent a good harvest. Not technically an herb, but still useful when used as one in magick.

Wormwood - for sending away. Use for causing an eviction, throwing out, or firing. Also use in reversal magick to send spells and hexes back to senders. CAUTION - known to be poisonous, avoid skin contact and store in a secure place.

Made in the USA
Las Vegas, NV
23 October 2024

10339698R00085